HOW TO DRAW
SUMMER THINGS
for kids

ALLI KOCH

Paige Tate & Co.

Copyright © 2025 Alli Koch
Published by Paige Tate & Co., an imprint of Blue Star Press
PO Box 8835, Bend, OR 97708
contact@paigetate.com
www.paigetate.com

All rights reserved. No part of this publication may be reproduced or transmitted in any form or by any means, electronic or mechanical, including photocopy, recording, or any information storage and retrieval system, without permission in writing from the publisher.

The authorized representative in the EU for product safety and compliance is Authorised Rep Compliance Ltd., Ground Floor, 71 Lower Baggot Street, Dublin D02 P593, Ireland. www.arccompliance.com

Written and illustrated by Alli Koch

ISBN: 9781963183290

Printed in Colombia

10 9 8 7 6 5 4 3 2 1

INTRO	5
TOOLS	6
BREAK IT DOWN	7
SUMMER THINGS	9
NATURE IN SUMMER	55
THE HOLIDAYS	67
CREATE YOUR OWN	75

LET'S DRAW!

The nice thing about being an artist is that you can make the rules. Everyone has their own style, which is why your drawings will look different from someone else's. In this book, each project is broken down into easy-to-follow steps. My goal is to help you see the simple parts of what may seem like a hard thing to draw.

We will start with the most basic outline or guide and work our way up. You will start to see a pattern with each summer thing we draw, starting with simple guidelines, then breaking down "C" and "S" shaped lines, and lastly erasing the unneeded lines for the finished look. Don't forget to draw your lines lightly first so it is easier to erase them. My favorite thing to say when drawing is:

If it was perfect, it would not look handmade!

I cannot wait for you to get started. Happy drawing!

TOOLS

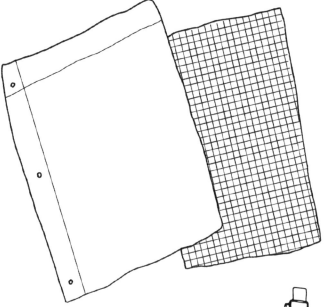

The cool thing about art is that you can use any tool you want! Yep, that's right! You are the artist, so feel free to be creative. For this book, let's keep it simple. It's easy to learn using either blank sheets of paper or grid paper.

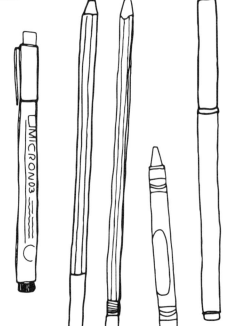

When you are learning to draw, you really only need a pencil and a good eraser. To follow the step-by-step instructions, draw everything lightly, then go over your lines with whatever tool you would like to use. You can use different pens, markers, colored pencils, or even crayons to add details to your drawings.

CIRCLES CAN BE TRICKY. TRY USING A PENNY OR A CIRCLE STENCIL TO HELP!

BREAK IT DOWN

Anyone can draw! If you can write your ABCs (which I am pretty sure you can do!), then you can draw everything in this book. Each project can be broken down into a bunch of "C" and "S" shaped lines. Almost anything that is round is two simple "C" shaped lines put together. An "S" shaped line is for when something has a dip or curvy line.

Most of the projects in this book are broken down into six or eight steps. What you need to draw in each step will appear as a black line; what you have already drawn will appear as gray lines. There are more than 40 summer-themed illustrations in this book for you to learn how to draw. The chapter dividers in this book are also bonus coloring pages that you can color!

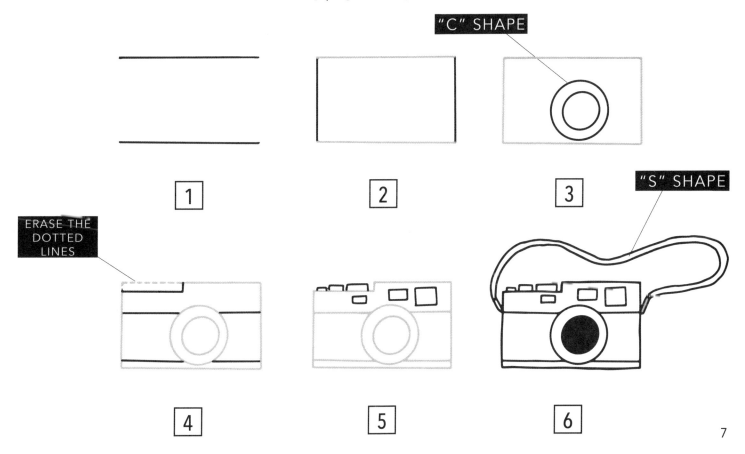

SUMMER THINGS

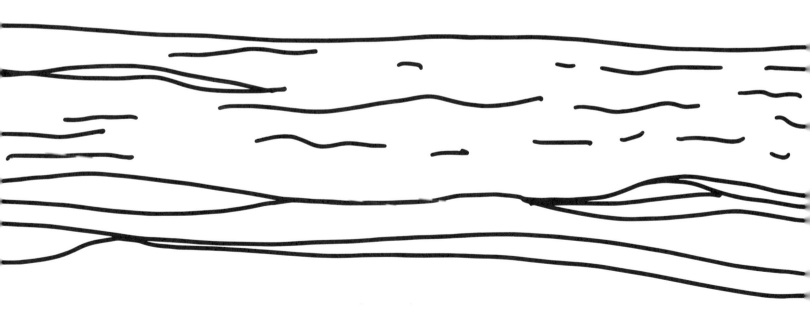

SWIMSUIT

In the early 1900s, people wore one-piece swimming costumes made of wool.

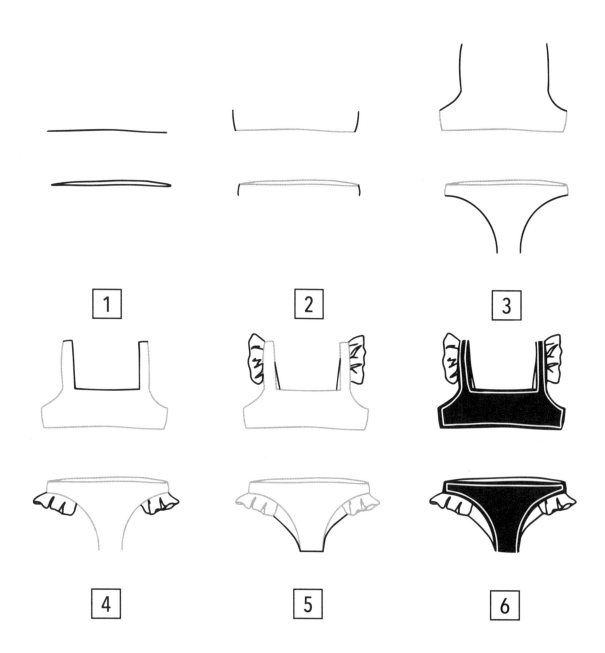

SWIMMING TRUNKS

In 1961, Carrie Birdwell Mann invented swimming trunks specifically made for surfing.

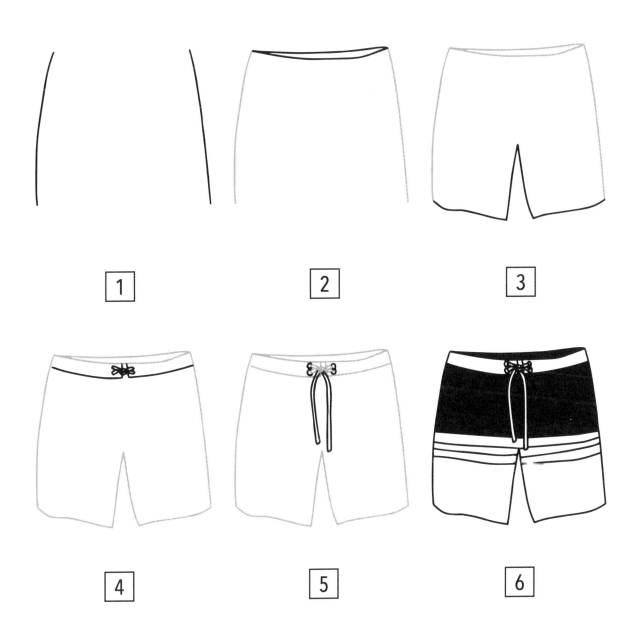

UMBRELLA

Umbrellas were first developed and used by ancient Egyptians to protect nobility and royalty from the sun's harsh rays.

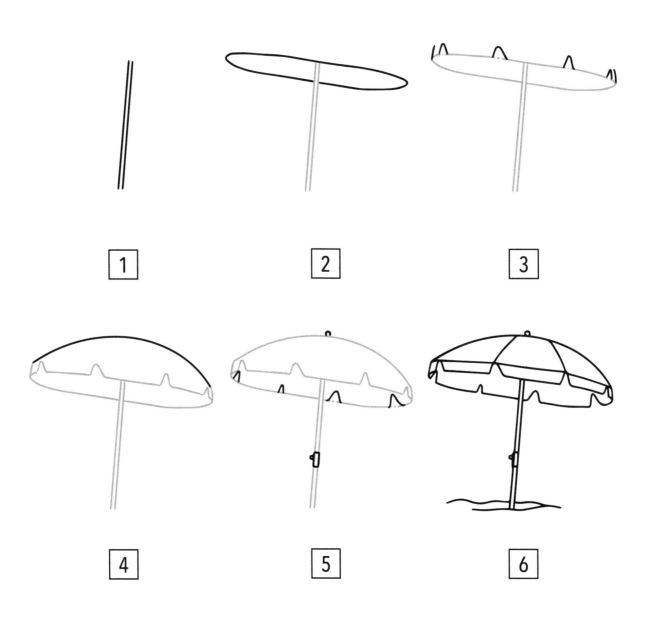

SNORKEL MASK

The word *snorkel* comes from the German word *schnorchel*, which means "snout."

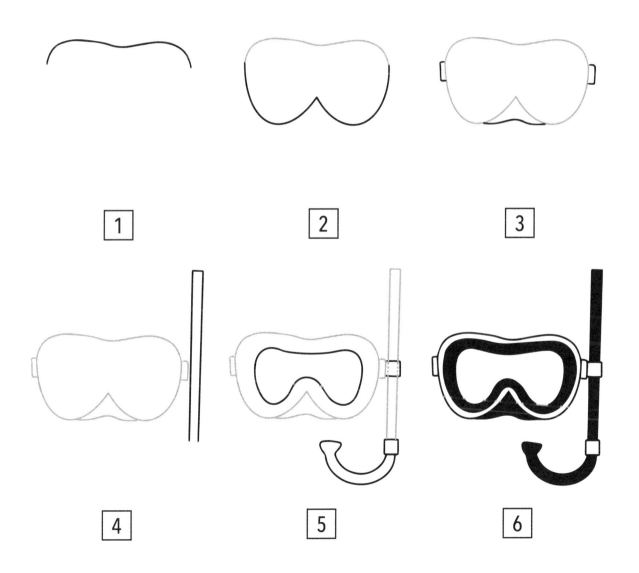

POOL FLOAT

Pool floats are made of a thin, synthetic material. Once inflated with air, the pool floats are less dense than water, which allows you to float with them on!

SUNGLASSES

On average, someone in America loses or breaks a pair of sunglasses every 14 minutes!

BOOM BOX

Boom boxes are portable sound systems that grew in popularity in the 1980s. Some boom boxes back then were as big as a suitcase!

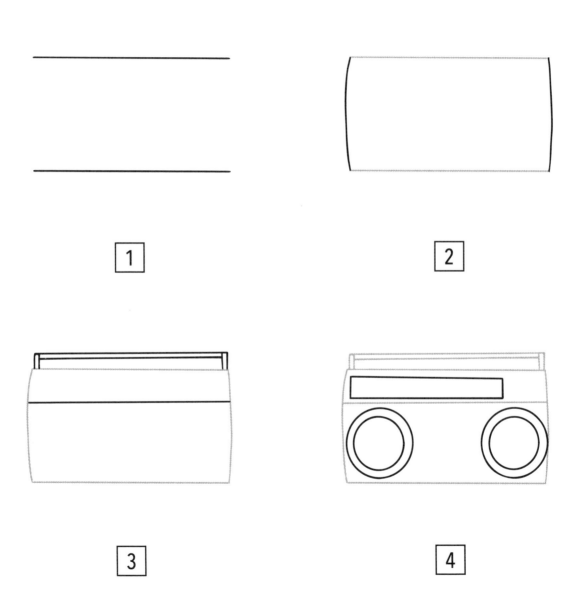

5

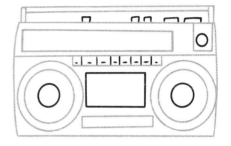

6

7

8

ROLLERBLADES

Did you know that rollerblading uses 80 percent of your body's muscles?

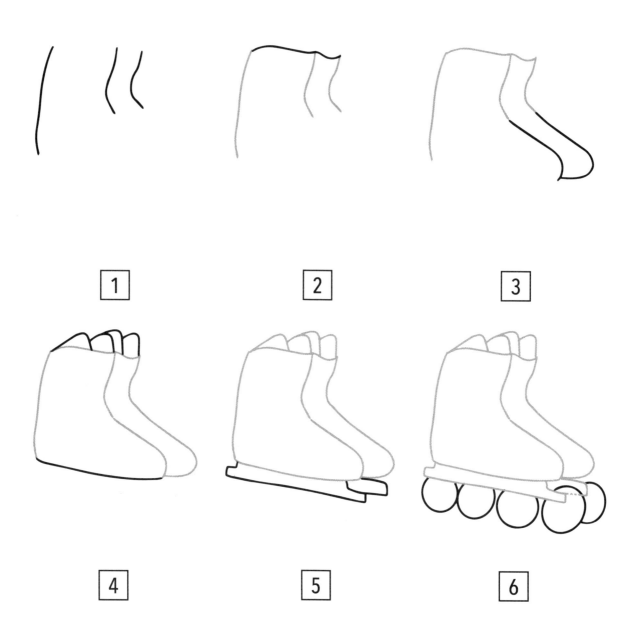

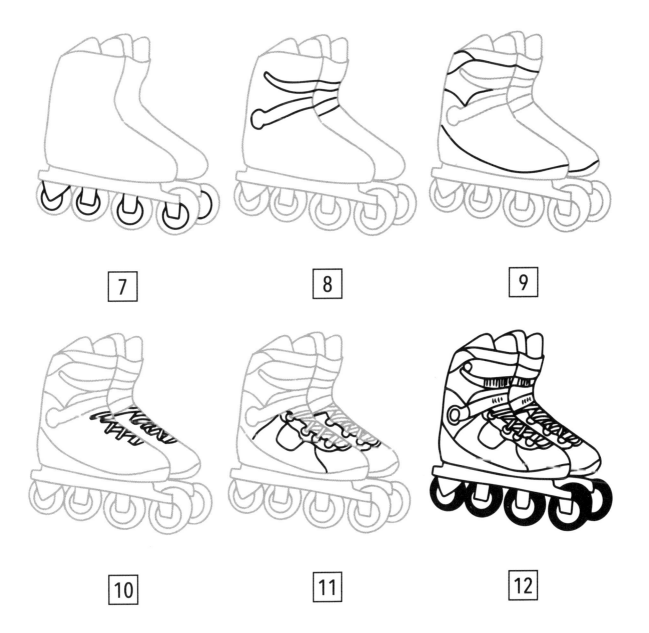

LAWN CHAIR

The first metal lawn chair with webbing was created by Fredric Arnold in 1947. A decade later, his company was manufacturing up to 14,000 lawn chairs a day.

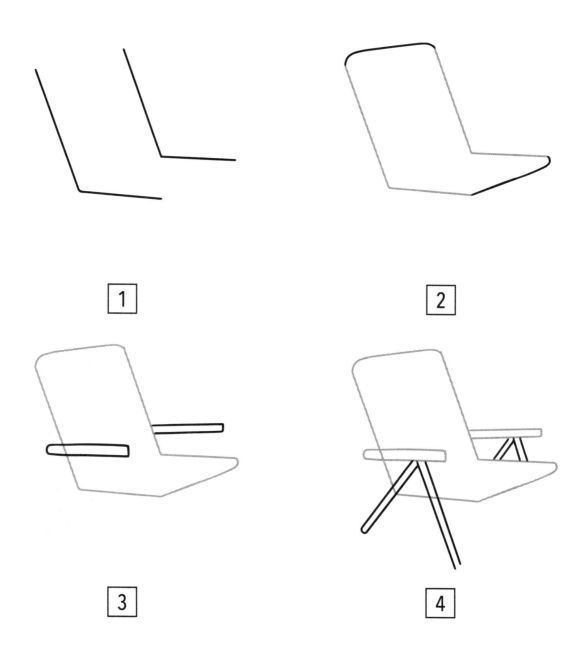

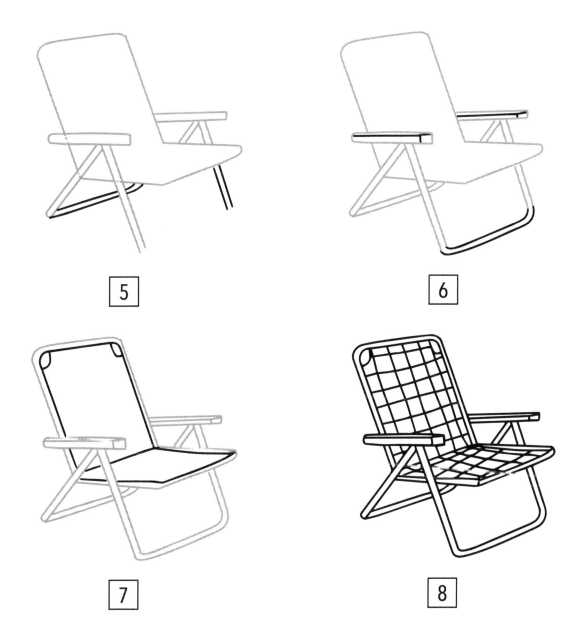

SANDCASTLE

The world's tallest sandcastle was built in Denmark in 2021 and measured almost 70 feet tall.

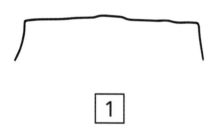

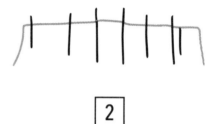

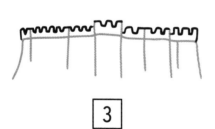

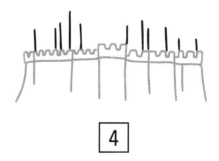

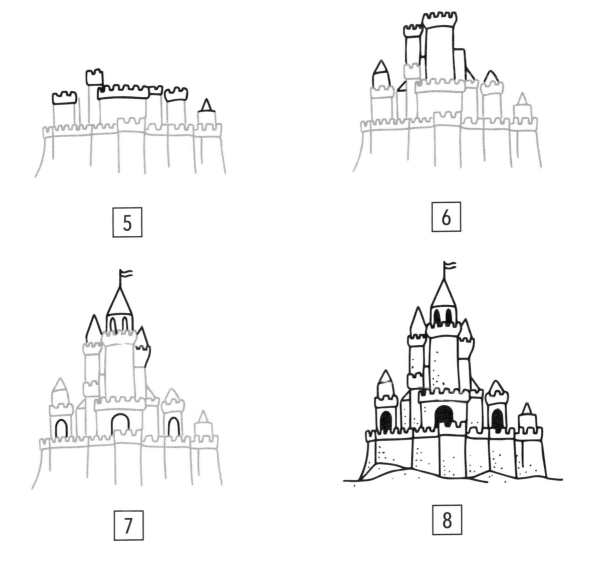

LIGHTHOUSE
The US has more lighthouses than any other country.

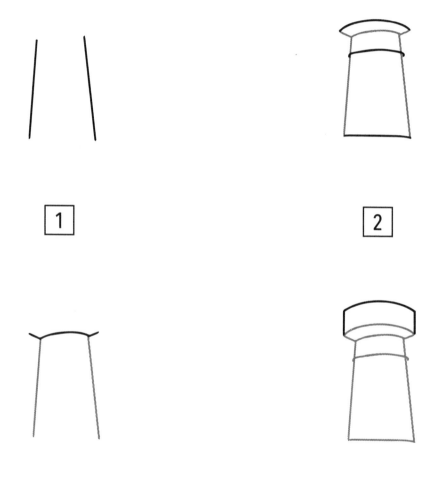

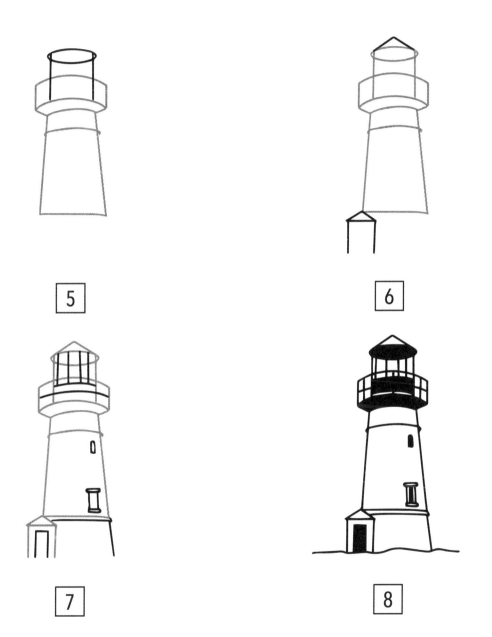

BOAT

The Spirit of Australia currently holds the record for the fastest boat in the world, reaching a speed of up to 317 mph.

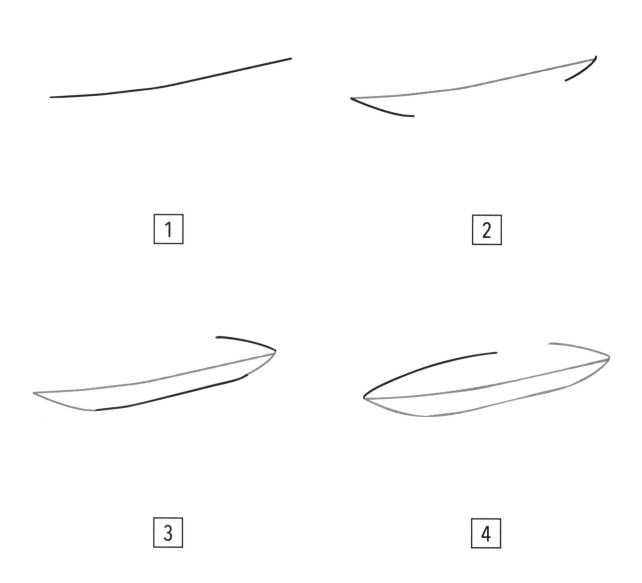

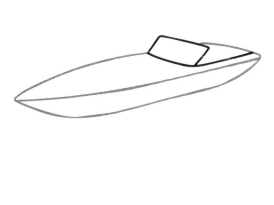

5

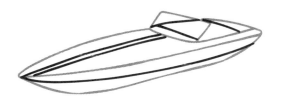

6

7

8

ICE CREAM

On average, it takes 50 licks to finish an ice cream cone.

BEACH BALL

The deeper a beach ball is pushed underwater, the faster it will pop back to the surface.

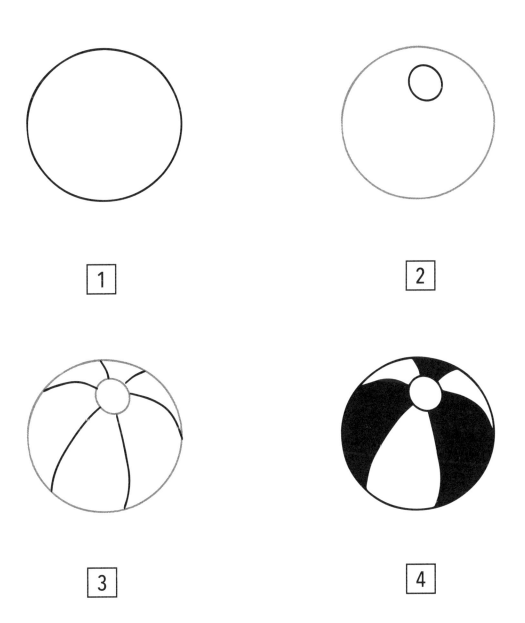

POPSICLE

In the winter of 1905, an eleven-year-old invented the popsicle by accident after he left a cup of soda with a stick inside it out on his porch.

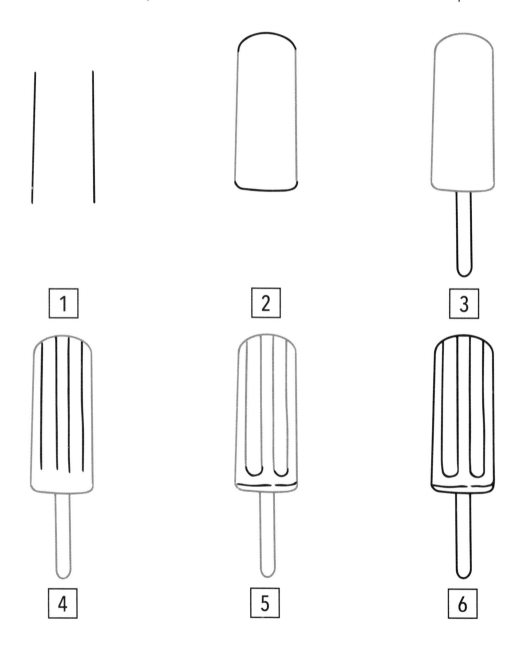

BEACH BAG

Beach bags are often made of water-resistant material, which means you can safely pack this book on your next beach trip!

SUN HAT

Sun hats are great for protecting your skin from the sun. They can even block 97 percent of the sun's UVB rays.

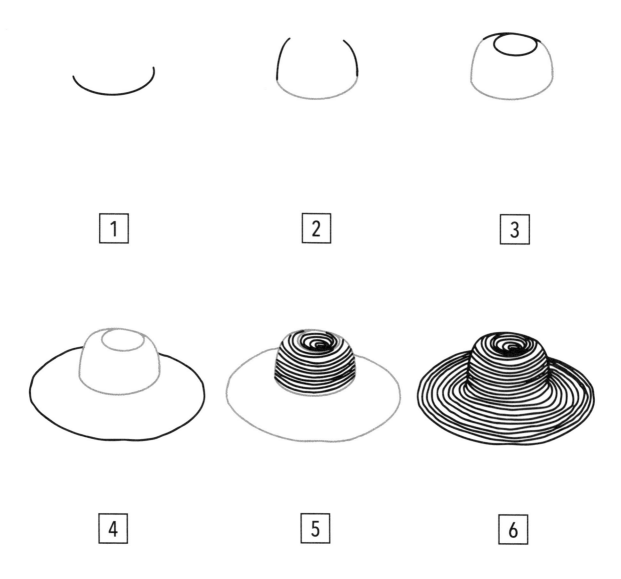

VISOR

Visors are a popular accessory when playing outdoor sports like tennis, golf, volleyball, and pickleball.

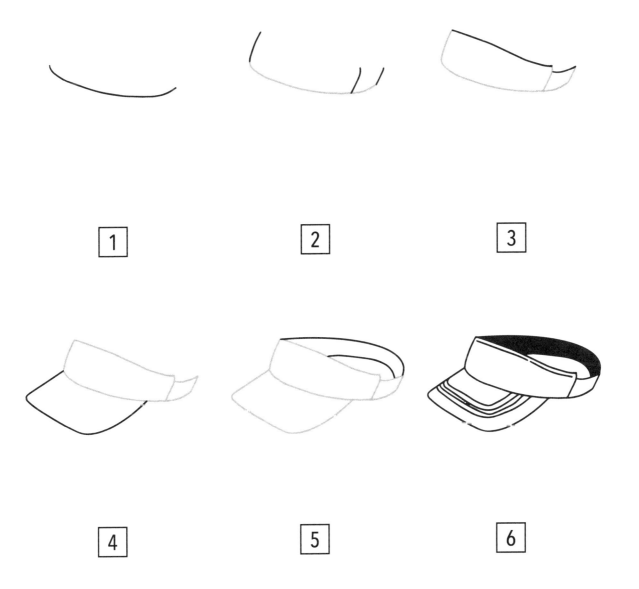

SURFBOARD

Archaeologists discovered carvings of people surfing that date back 5,000 years, making it one of the world's oldest sports!

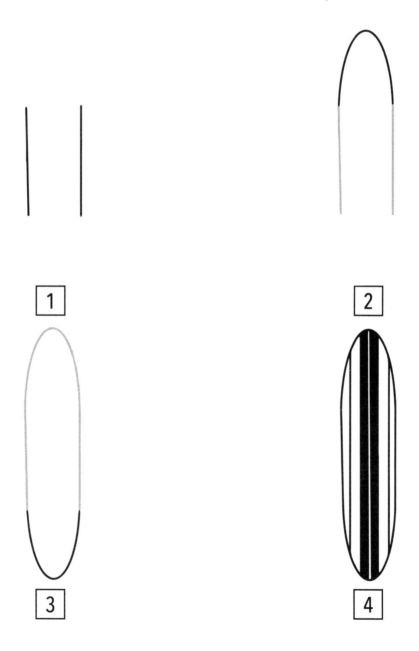

SUNSCREEN

Because it takes time for your skin to absorb sunscreen, it's recommended to wait at least 30 minutes between putting on sunscreen and going outside.

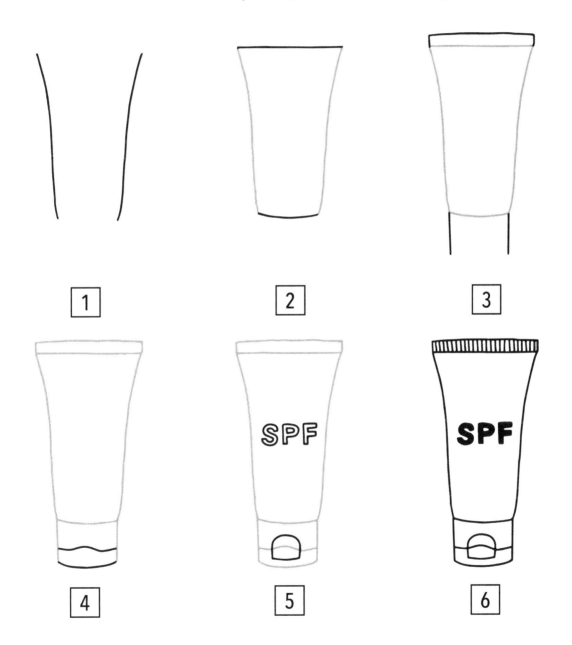

PICNIC BASKET

During the Victorian era, picnics were often intricate meals that included foods like duck, lobster, and tongue. What foods would you take on your dream picnic?

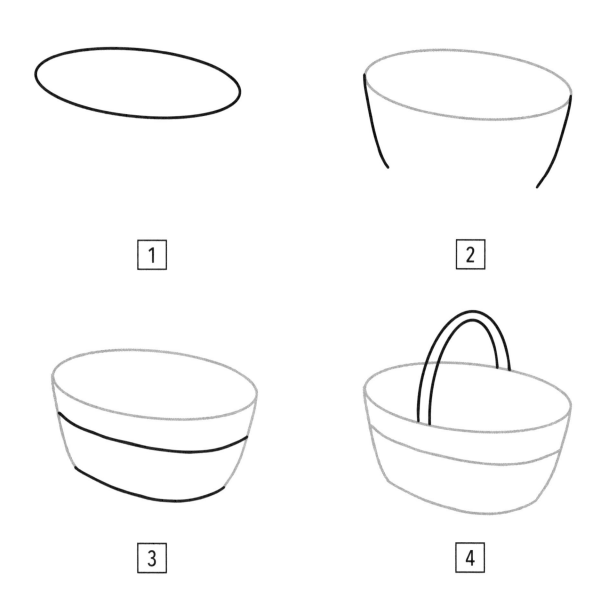

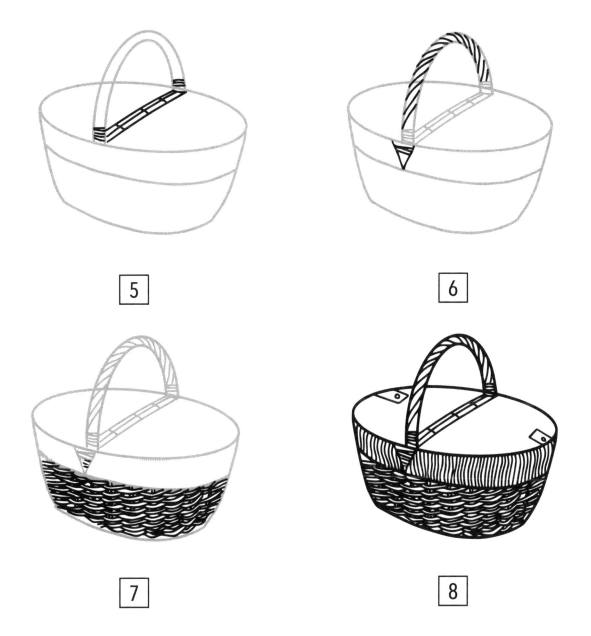

BBQ GRILL

The word *barbecue* originally comes from *barbacoa*, which is the Taíno tribe's word for "grilling on wood."

1

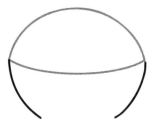

2

3

4

HOT DOG

Hot dogs were one of the first foods to be eaten on the moon.

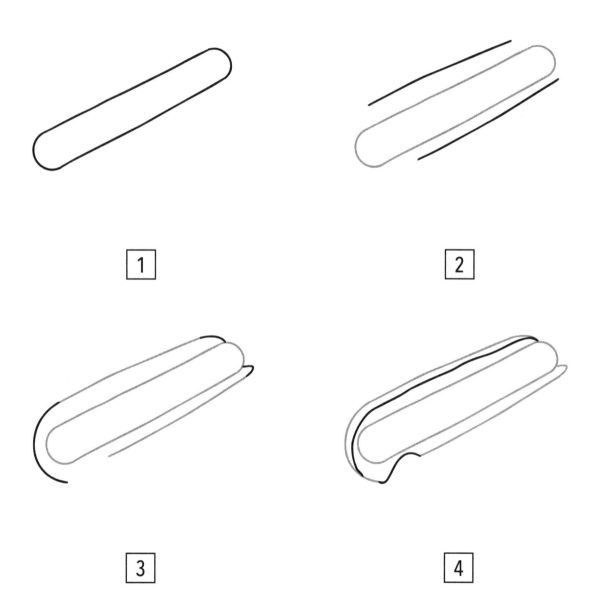

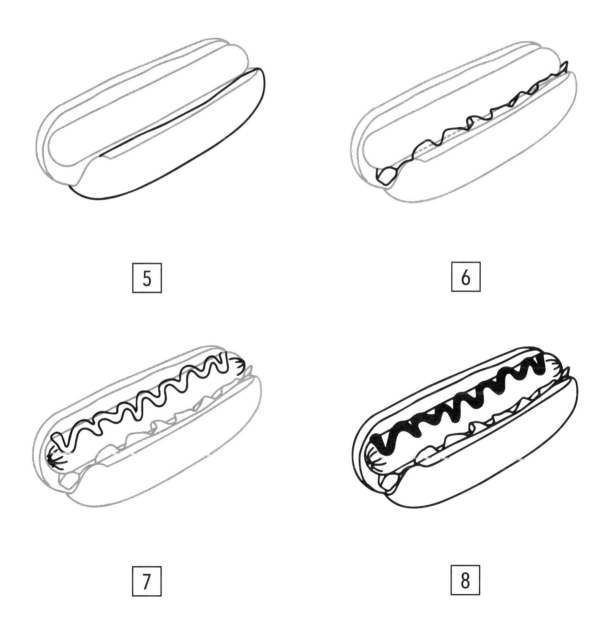

HAMBURGER

The United States Department of Agriculture estimates that Americans eat 50 billion hamburgers each year.

CHERRIES

Cherries are a natural source of melatonin, which is something that can help you sleep!

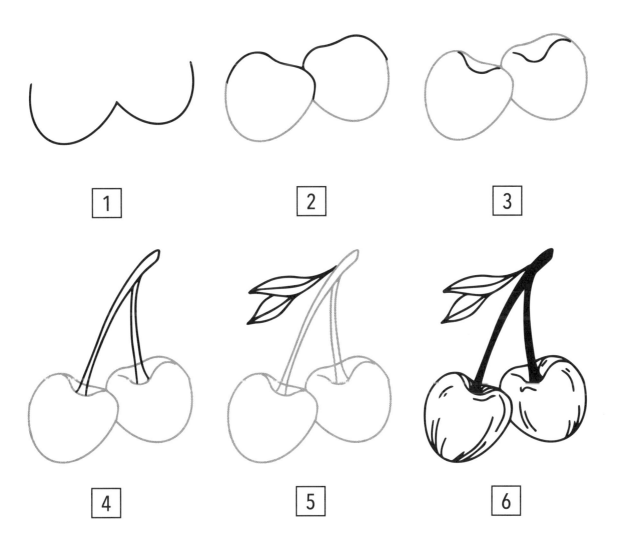

LEMONADE

Research suggests that the sour flavor in lemonade can actually be thirst-quenching. No wonder lemonade is so refreshing on a hot summer's day!

WATERMELON

Watermelon is a good source of potassium, which is a nutrient that helps your muscles and heart function properly.

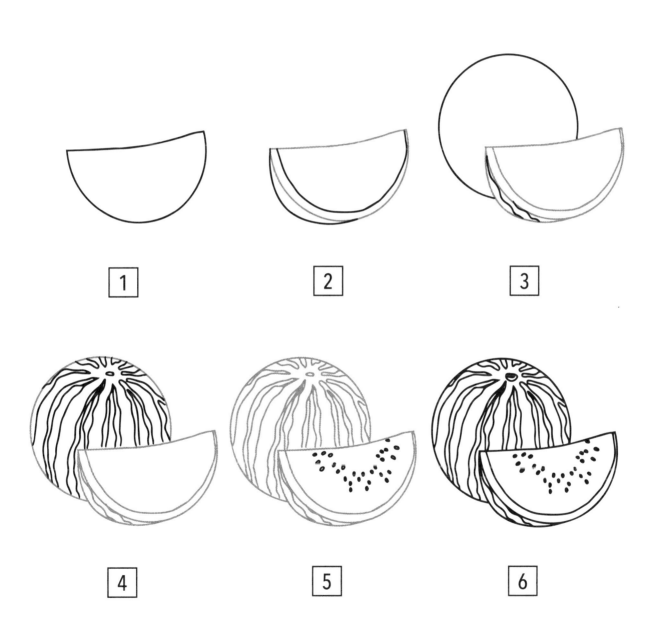

SUITCASE

Originally made from wood or leather, suitcases used to be very heavy and difficult to carry.

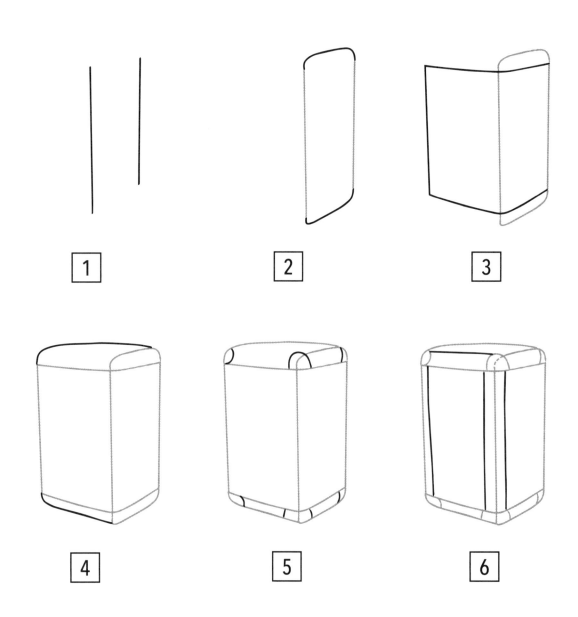

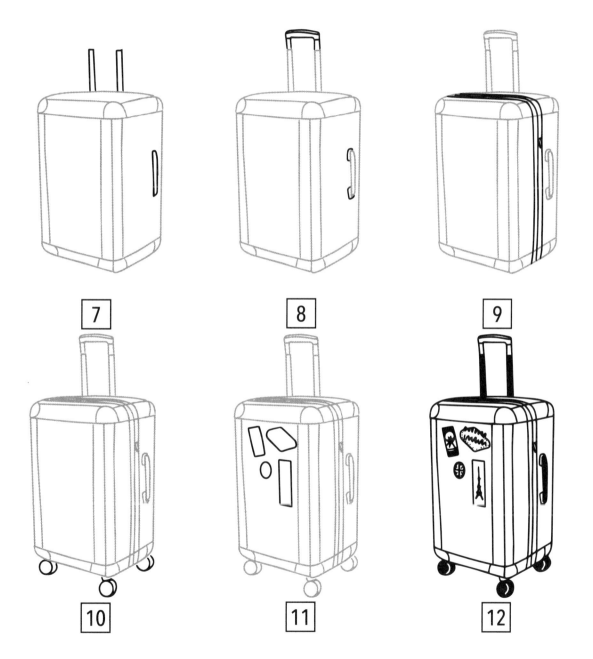

AIRPLANE

Planes are designed to be able to withstand lightning strikes.

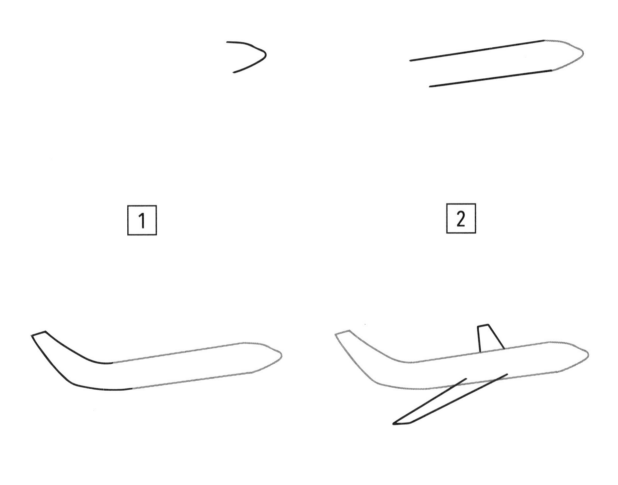

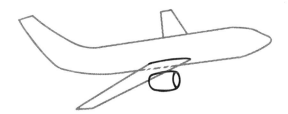

5

6

7

8

JEEP

The Jeep played an integral role in America's efforts in World War II. It even received a Purple Heart—the only American vehicle to do so!

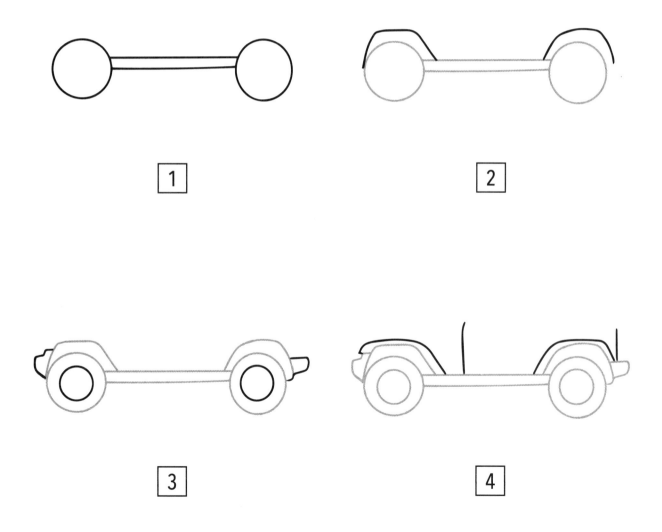

BIKE

It's estimated that one billion people ride bikes each day. That's almost one in every eight people!

5

6

7

8

SUNFLOWER

Sunflowers move to face the sun as it rises and sets throughout the day. This behavior is called *heliotropism*.

[1]

[2]

[3]

[4]

CACTUS

The saguaro cactus can live to be up to 200 years old and grow to be 50 feet tall.

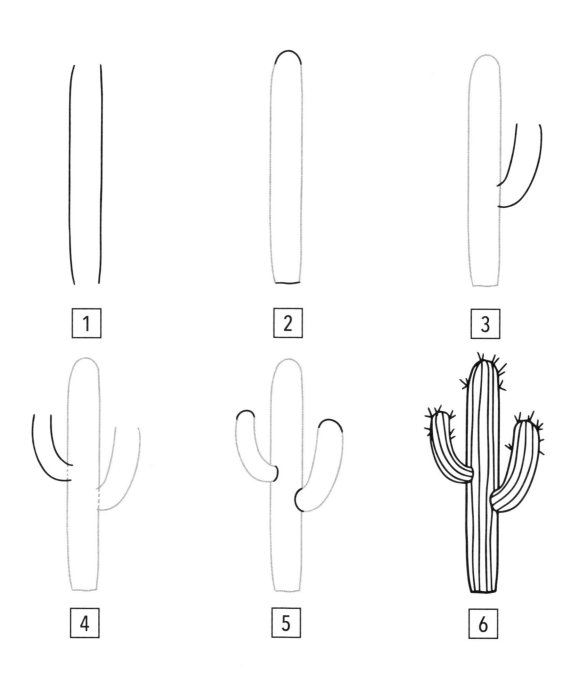

PALM TREE

There are more than 2,500 species of palm trees in the world.

FLAMINGO

Flamingos build their nests out of mud and other small materials, like feathers and stones.

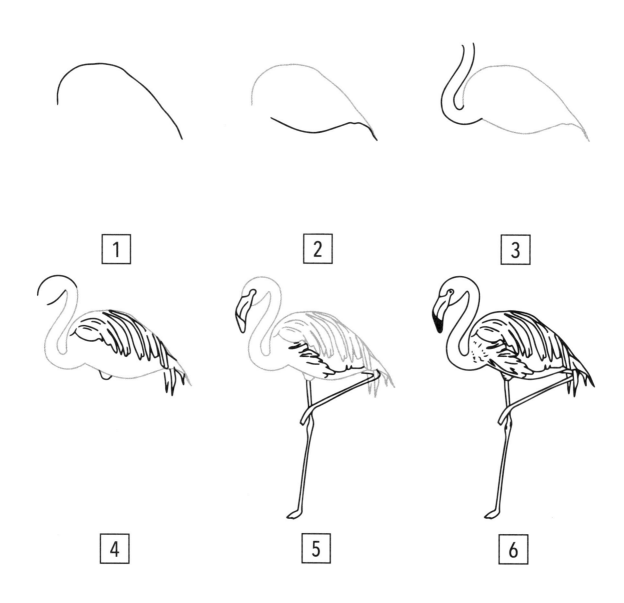

SEAGULL

The color of a seagull's beak can change depending on their age and what they eat.

CRAB

Measuring 12 feet in width, the Japanese spider crab is the world's largest crab.

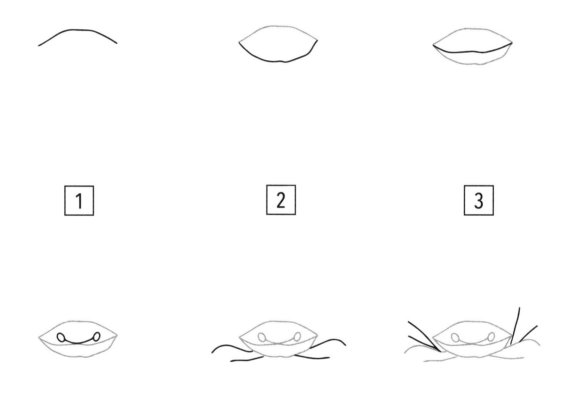

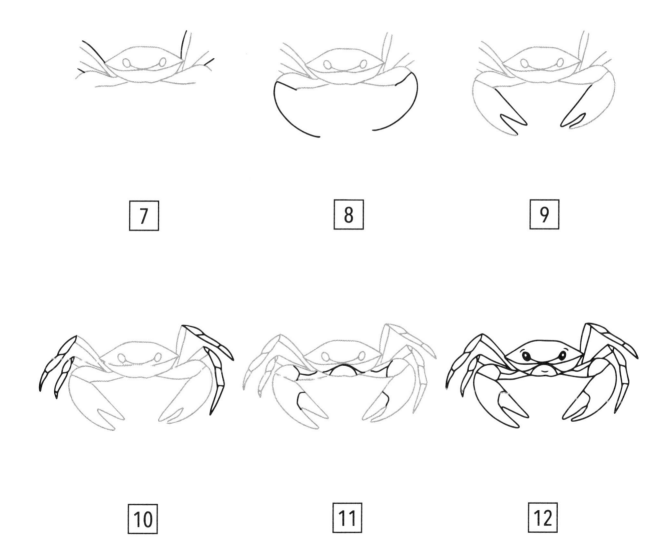

SEASHELLS

Ninety percent of seashells open to the right, like the one on page 65. If you find a seashell that opens to the left, it's considered to be very rare!

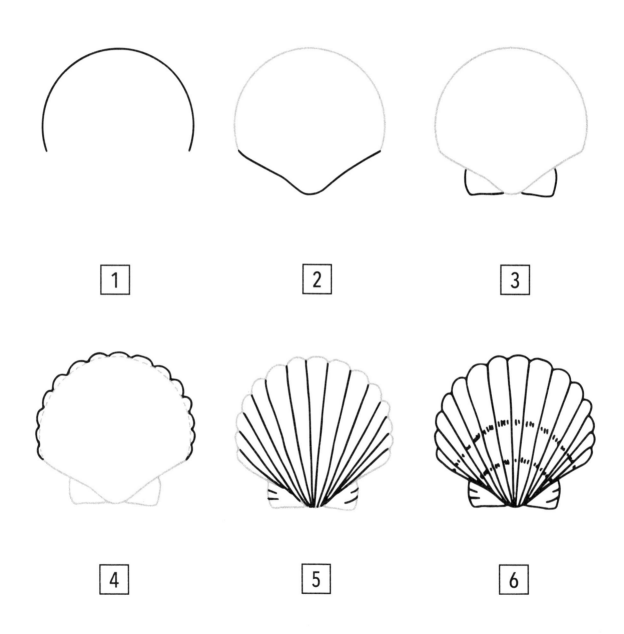

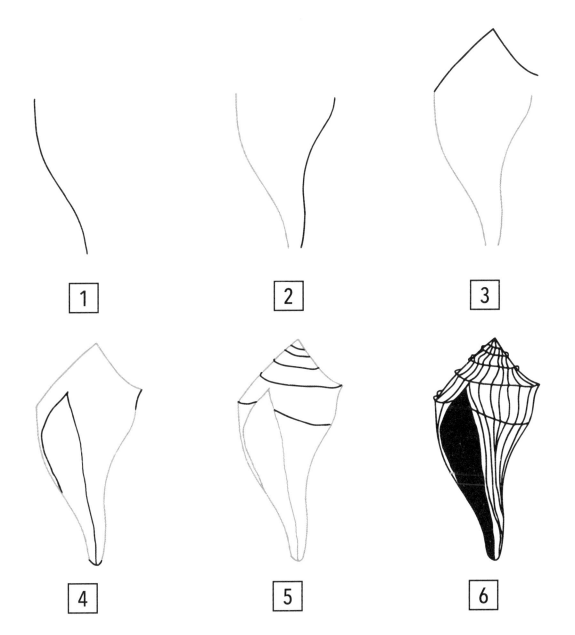

THE HOLIDAYS

AMERICAN FLAG

The fifty stars on the American flag represent the fifty states. Can you name them all?

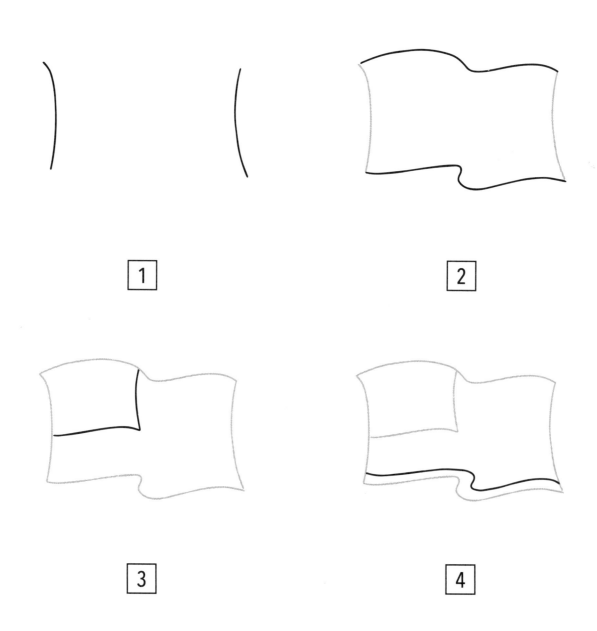

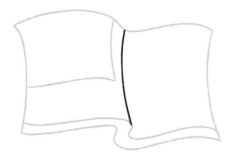

5

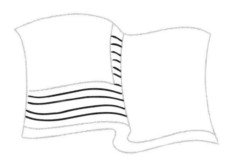

6

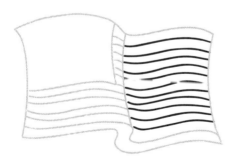

7

8

FIREWORKS

Americans have been setting off fireworks to celebrate independence for centuries. They even set off fireworks on the very first Independence Day on July 4, 1777.

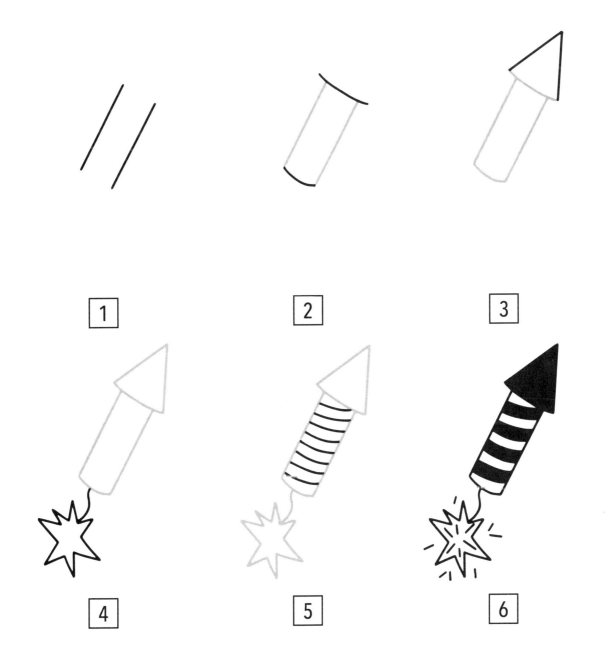

TOP HAT

It's believed that the first top hat was created in 1793.

PINWHEEL

In the 1800s, pinwheels were also called "whirligigs."

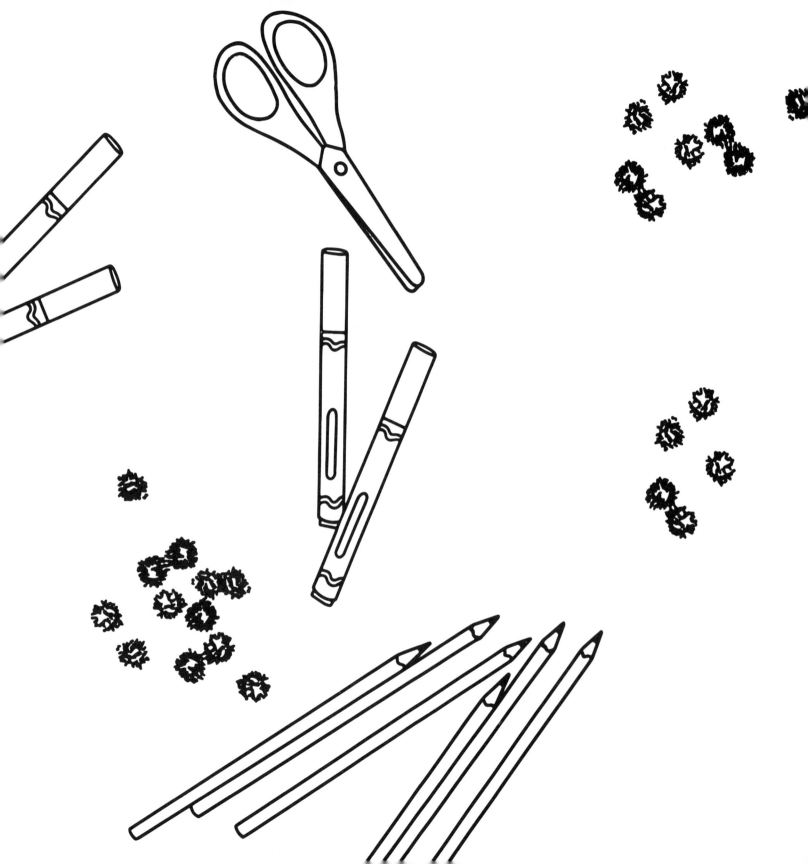

CREATE YOUR OWN

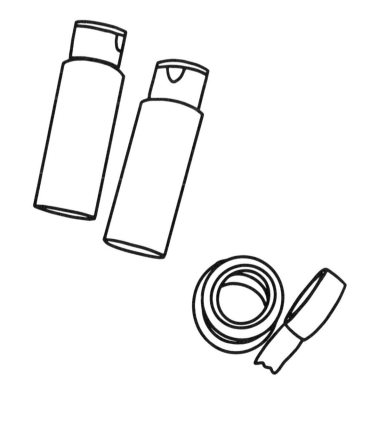

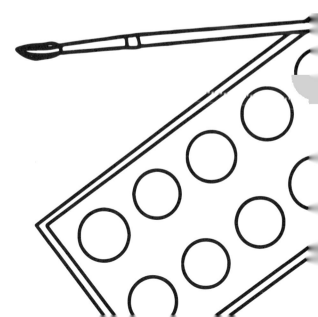

CREATE YOUR OWN ICE CREAM

Use this page to create your favorite ice cream cone!

CREATE YOUR OWN POOL PARTY

Use this page to draw your own pool party!

About Alli K

NAME: Alli Koch

HOME: Dallas, Texas

BIRTHDAY: March 20, 1991

FAVORITE COLOR: Black

FAVORITE FOOD: Waffle fries and a large sweet tea

JOB: I am a full-time artist! I sell my art online, paint murals on the sides of buildings, and teach others how to draw or be creative

SUMMER FAVORITE: Riding around in my Jeep with the roof off

PETS: I have one cat named Emmie

CAR: Two-door Jeep

FAMILY: Married to my high school sweetheart

FAVORITE THING TO DO: Play board games!